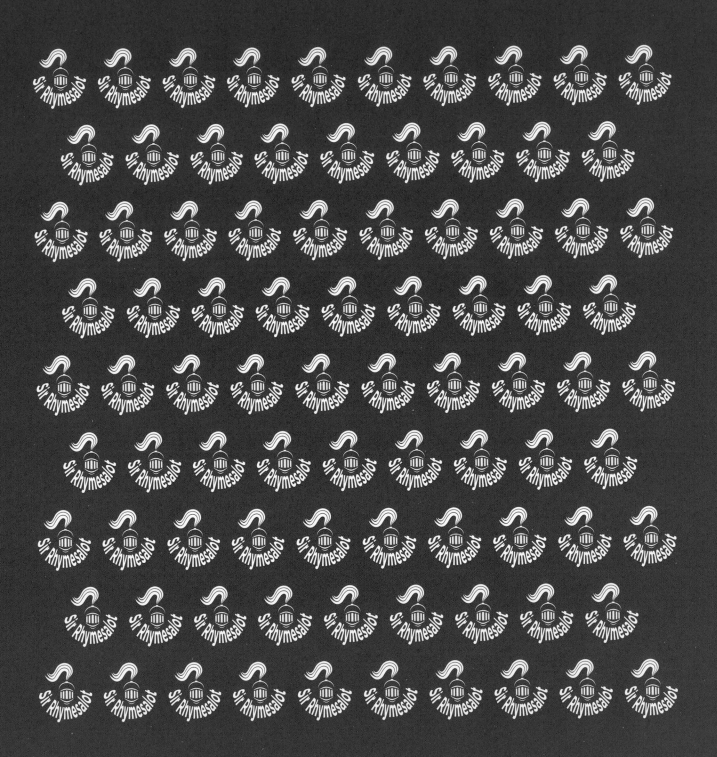

I LOST MY BRAVE

The big bully birthday

Sir Rhymesalot

This book contains rhyming
Tools. Scan the QR code to
find out how they work.

I woke up excited
the day was now here.
I'd waited, and waited,
and waited all year.
My friends will all come,
soon they'll arrive.
It's a really big deal,
today I turn five!

Four was ok,
I had a good time.
I learned a few things,
like reading and rhyme.
I learned how to count,
I made some new friends.
But five is no-nonsense,
I'm halfway to ten.

Showered and shaved,
'though my beard's not yet grown.
I use shaving cream
and the back of my comb.
My dad showed me how,
I practice each day.
So when there's hairs there
I can keep them at bay.

My party's at 3
so I still have some time.
Mom's baking cake,
and choc-dipped madeleines.
Dad has a plan
for some games we can play.
A three-legged race,
Tug-of-war, and charades.

Sometimes I get worried,
and I just recalled why.
Bradley is coming,
and he's not a nice guy.
My parents are friends
with his mom and dad.
So Bradley's invited
and he makes me feel bad.

When we go to the playground
and the parents are busy.
He pushes me down,
one time I got dizzy.
He punches my arms,
it's no way to behave.
I want to fight back
but I lost all my brave.

Now I am nervous,
how could this be?
What if he hits me,
and all my friends see!
All my excitement
was draining from me.
I wish that my birthday
did not include Bradley.

My mom sees me thinking,
she looks right at me.
She says, "you look down,
is there something you need?"
"There is," I said,
somewhat hesitantly.
"I'm a bit scared of Bradley,
he's so mean to me."

"I will be watching,
don't worry, my darling.
Nothing will hurt you,
not even his snarling."
"Snarling?" I thought,
"How could this be!
My mother's aware
of this controversy?"

"A bully won't bully
just to be mean.
The problem with bullies
is low self-esteem.
I too was bullied,"
my mom said to me.
"But I talked to that bully
and helped him to see."

3 o'clock came,
the first guests arrived
My palms started sweating,
I felt terrified.
At a quarter to four,
came a knock at the door.
Bradley said gladly
"I've come back for more."

"Brad," I said sternly.
"I know what is wrong.
You just want some friends,
you want to belong.
I'll be your friend,
but there has to be rules.
You stop being mean,
and we will be cool.

If you hit me or call me
bad names you can beat it.
Treat me the way
you would like to be treated.
Bradley was shocked,
he stood very still.
His mouth was wide open,
he was looking quite ill.

I suddenly noticed
how quiet it was.
My friends were all frozen,
like someone hit pause.
I wasn't aware
that everyone heard.
They started to clap,
they'd heard every word.

Bradley was stunned
but he started to smile.
"That sounds good to me,
if I can stay for a while."
The party was grand,
in five years, I'll turn ten.
And Bradley and I,
May become best of friends.

Scan this QR code with your phone camera
for more titles from imagine and wonder

Your guarantee of quality

As publishers, we strive to produce every book to the highest commercial standards. The printing and binding have been planned to ensure a sturdy, attractive publication which should give years of enjoyment.

Replacement assurance

If your copy fails to meet our high standards, please inform us and we will gladly replace it.
admin@imagineandwonder.com

Printed in China by Hung Hing Off-set Printing Co. Ltd.

Scan the QR code to find other
Sir Rhymesalot books and more from
www.ImagineAndWonder.com

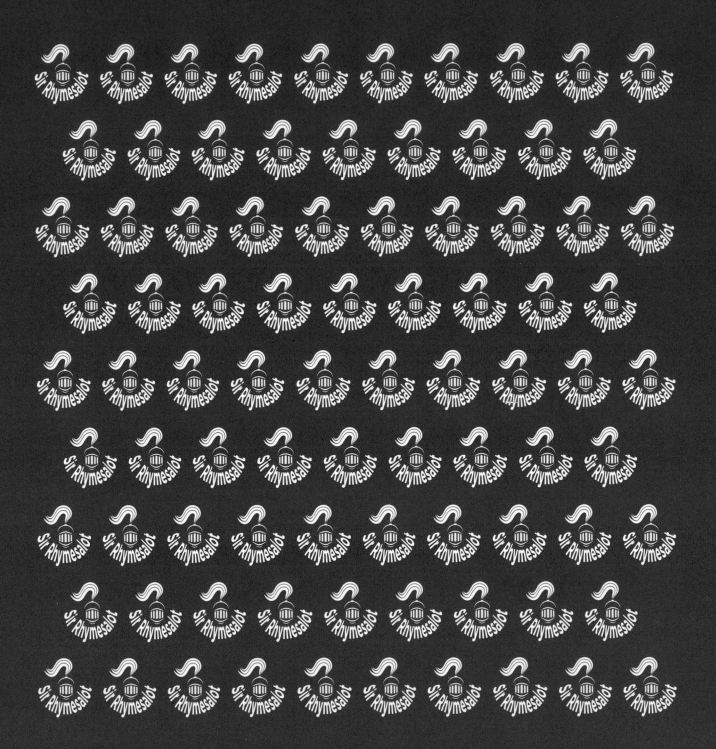